Original title:
The House of My Heart

Copyright © 2025 Creative Arts Management OÜ
All rights reserved.

Author: Dorian Ashford
ISBN HARDBACK: 978-1-80587-162-0
ISBN PAPERBACK: 978-1-80587-632-8

Garden of Unfurling Wishes

In a patch of dreams, flowers bloom,
Dandelions dance, chasing the gloom.
Whimsical gnomes with grins so wide,
Play hide and seek, in a sunny slide.

A butterfly flits, with a top hat on,
Sipping sweet nectar from dawn till dawn.
Wishes are weeds in a comical race,
Sprouting in laughter, all over the place.

Gallery of Treasured Moments

Photos hang crooked, on the bright wall,
Each goofy grin, a memory's call.
Grandma's cat wearing sunglasses cool,
Is the star of the show, breaking all rules.

A collage of chaos, laughter's delight,
Balloons that popped in a comical fright.
Every snapshot, a tale to tell,
In this quirky gallery, all is quite swell.

Portals to My Inner Sanctuary

Doors that squeak like a cartoon rabbit,
Lead me to dreams that are fun and habbit.
A closet with socks, colorful and bright,
Dancing around in the soft moonlight.

Mirrors that giggle when I pass by,
Reflecting my worries, waving them goodbye.
Inside the wardrobe, old hats laugh loud,
Cheering for joy, a whimsical crowd.

The Quiet of My Spirit's Retreat

Under the blanket fort, treasures reside,
A sandwich half-eaten, my secret pride.
Monsters under the bed, wearing fuzzy socks,
Trading their roars for soft, gentle knocks.

In this sweet bubble, silence ticks slow,
Pillow fights with shadows and giggles that flow.
Each tickle of laughter, a spark ignites,
In this cozy corner, everything feels right.

Touchstones of Longing Hearts

In a mansion filled with socks,
I trip over dino toys.
The kitchen sings with laughter,
While I chase the garlic boys.

Pizza nights and cake in sight,
Pajamas rule the floor.
Can't find my other shoe tonight,
But hey, who keeps score?

Echoed Lullabies Through Time

Old clocks chime at 3 AM,
Then snore like a bear.
Kids sleepwalk like pros,
While I ponder my hair.

The old cat's tail is my guide,
As I tiptoe downstairs.
I miss the days of sleeping wide,
Now I dance with my cares.

Sills Adorned with Quiet Hope

Little plants on window sills,
Grew like my dreams of cake.
They stretch, they bend, they spill their frills,
Cuz hey, what's at stake?

Balloons float by the garden gate,
Chasing dust bunnies too.
A day where chores can wait,
Is like winning the flu!

Reflections on Polished Floors

These shiny tiles reflect my feet,
As I dance in pure delight.
Each chaotic spin's a treat,
In this absurd highlight.

Sliding with a woosh and grin,
Like penguins on a spree.
Life's a funny game we win,
With spills and glee, you see!

Nooks of Forgotten Laughter

In corners where the shadows play,
A crumpled joke has come to stay.
The cat laughs at the chair's old tale,
While the clock ticks on, quite pale.

Mismatched socks and cereal spoons,
Dance around like disco tunes.
Chairs wear years like comfy pants,
And dreams still waltz with none but chance.

Old books grin with wisdom's tease,
While hidden squirrels relax with ease.
In laughter's nooks, time takes a dive,
Where silly memories come alive.

Pathways to Inner Tranquility

The path is strewn with rubber ducks,
Amidst the laughter, joy erupts.
Flip-flops squeak on tiles that shine,
As my thoughts and giggles intertwine.

With every step, a chuckle blooms,
As rabbit slippers dance in rooms.
Garden gnomes in shades of bright,
Join in on this goofy plight.

Sunflowers wink with silly stance,
In all of nature's quirky dance.
Winding roads of jovial cheer,
Lead to peace when you venture near.

Hearth of Warm Embraces

The fire crackles with witty jest,
While marshmallows toast and make a mess.
Warmth that smells like burnt delight,
S'mores and smiles fill the night.

Grandma's recipes are full of spice,
But her jokes? Oh, they're not so nice!
With every laugh, the shadows flee,
As the scent of cookies gets to me.

Pillow forts gather dust and dreams,
As laughter bubbles in hilarious streams.
Cozy spots where silliness blooms,
And every corner beckons, 'Zoom!'

Windows to My Deepest Yearnings

Peeking through a curtain's sway,
I spy a dance party made of clay.
With silly hats and bouncing shoes,
Who knew yearning had such grooves?

Window boxes filled with socks,
Graffiti hearts and ticking clocks.
As wishes float on wobbly chairs,
My dreams take flight on imaginary flares.

The world outside seems far away,
But inside, giggles pave the way.
With every glance through crystal panes,
A heartful chuckle gently reigns.

The Weight of Lovelorn Walls

There's a door that never shuts,
It squeaks like my old dog.
The windows wink at passersby,
Whispering tales of my fog.

A fridge that only hums bad tunes,
With magnets lining up like friends.
It dances, rumbles, and misbehaves,
Claiming love never quite ends.

The floors are sticky, filled with crumbs,
From breakfasts we never had.
Each step a slapstick comedy,
Still making me laugh, not sad.

There's a closet stuffed with old regrets,
Hats from parties long ago.
They all laugh out loud at my plans,
Yet I still invite them to the show.

Fragrant Blooms of Shared Smiles

In the kitchen, love brews strong,
Coffee spills like laughter shared.
Sugar fights with the milk jug,
Telling secrets, none prepared.

The pantry's full of wild snacks,
Chips whisper stories of the past.
Each crunch, a giggle in the air,
Munching memories, unsurpassed.

Baking bombs from a clumsy chef,
Flour clouds like winter's snow.
Cookies shape-shift into silly forms,
Making sure my heart's aglow.

Yet blooms with laughter fill my rooms,
Potted plants with cheeky grins.
Their leaves sway in the breezy fun,
Celebrating life and all its wins.

Gardens of Infinite Possibilities

In the backyard, weeds are wild,
Giggling flowers, oh so free.
They dance in circles, make me smile,
Roots entwined in silly glee.

Garden gnomes with clueless looks,
Watching bees play hopscotch here.
Their ceramic faces cracked with glee,
Confirming that all's well, my dear.

Rakes and shovels play hide and seek,
Underneath a bush of sass.
Each time I bend to peek around,
They shove me down, full of class.

Every corner has a joke to tell,
With every seed I've ever sown.
In this patch of jumbled joy,
My heart finds a home all its own.

Shadows of Gentle Comfort

In corners where socks go to hide,
There's laughter and giggles, side by side.
A cat on the windowsill plots and schemes,
While dust bunnies dance in my wildest dreams.

Cushions that swallow my stress and strife,
Whispers of joy from each corner of life.
Under the table, a treasure trove waits,
Chocolates and crumbs, oh how my heart mates!

Enclaves of Hopeful Reflection

Mirror, mirror, don't be so sly,
Have you seen my last slice of pie?
With a wink and a grin, it flies from the plate,
I'll find it again—promise, I'll wait!

The fridge hums a tune so sweet,
Echoing laughter with each little beat.
What hidden delights are waiting for me?
A midnight snack? Oh, it's meant to be!

Threads of Woven Sentiment

A quilt on the couch, oh what a feat,
Stitched with memories of stories and treats.
Each patch tells a tale of mishaps and fun,
Like the time I tripped while chasing the sun.

Grandma's old slippers, they're worn and quite dear,
One's missing a toe, but I hold them near.
In this cozy nook of silly delight,
Sleepovers with popcorn, we'd laugh into night.

Beams of Unseen Love

Sun beams sneak in, tickling my toes,
Turning my worries to giggles, who knows?
The kettle hops like it's ready to cheer,
And dances around with a whistle so clear.

With friends gathered 'round for a blender of fun,
Smoothies and stories—yup, we're all one.
In this quirky abode, joy flutters free,
Like a marshmallow ghost—just me and my tea!

Lanterns of Guiding Spirits

In a cottage where socks are lost,
The cat claims the couch at any cost.
Wandering gnomes with silly hats,
Dance with the mice and sip on sprats.

The fridge buzzes like a happy bee,
Where ketchup flows like the deep blue sea.
Ghosts tell jokes in the misty air,
Spinning funny tales without a care.

Each spoon is a wand, each bowl a throne,
Pasta noodles are twirled like a hone.
Laughter echoes off the walls,
As candy canes spring from all the halls.

So raise your glass of fizzy cheer,
To spinning teapots and hearty beer.
In this place where spirits prance,
Every day is a silly dance.

Stones Set in Heartfelt Paths

Pebbles laugh as you trip and slide,
They know all the secrets you try to hide.
Giggling stones in a wobbly row,
Guide your feet when you steal the show.

A snail parade moves with great flair,
Waving tiny flags, tossing bits of hair.
Nature's jesters in a grand parade,
On this twisting path, both bold and swayed.

Dandelions wink with mischievous glee,
As you dodge the weeds, they tickle your knee.
Each stone whispers a joke or a pun,
Under the shining, hot summer's sun.

So stomp along with clumsy grace,
Wear that smudge of dirt, a badge, not a trace.
Every stumble is part of the art,
On this silly trek, straight from the heart.

Celestial Ceilings of Shared Dreams

Under a ceiling of sparkling lights,
Dreams float around like silly kites.
Stars play tricks like mischievous sprites,
Winking down on our cozy nights.

The moon wears a hat that's far too big,
While planets dance a hilarious jig.
Galaxies giggle in twinkling fashion,
Each flash a blast of joyful passion.

Comets race, taking off with a grin,
Chasing each other, let the fun begin!
Nebulas swirl in bright, fuzzy hues,
Painting the sky with whimsical views.

So gather 'round for a celestial feast,
With laughter and joy that never cease.
In this dreamy realm of giggles and beams,
We're all just stardust chasing our dreams.

Routes Traveling to the Core

On a map crafted from coffee stains,
Every path leads to silly gains.
With squiggly lines that twist and turn,
Each journey beckons with much to learn.

A road that's paved with jelly beans,
Where laughter echoes and silly scenes.
Cars made of gumdrop and fuzzy fur,
Zoom through puddles with a happy blur.

Each corner brings a surprise or two,
Clowns in the bushes and dancing shrews.
Navigating through giggles and glee,
Is the secret to joyous discovery.

So hop aboard for a ride so bright,
Where every wrong turn feels just right.
In this land of laughter and colorful lore,
Every route leads straight to the core.

Mosaics of Passionate Affection

In a cozy nook where love resides,
Laughter bounces off the walls,
We feast on cookies, quite the prize,
The dog just tripped; oh, how he falls!

Socks all scattered, like puzzle pieces,
Whispers shared in giggles bright,
Dancing shadows, joy increases,
Did I mention? I lost a fight!

Tea-stained carpets tell our tales,
With silly hats and failed ballet,
Each moment sparks; no room for fails,
We dance in chaos; let's par-tay!

Balloons and banter fill the air,
I swear we're making memories,
A chandelier? No, just a pear,
With friends like these, life's a tease!

Labyrinths of Inner Exploration

Down the hall of silly dreams,
I lost my keys—who'd hide them so?
Chasing shadows, nothing's as it seems,
Reality? Hardly, but just go with the flow.

A mirror maze of smiles and frowns,
I thought I'd found some hidden gold,
Turns out it's just my old clown gown,
I really need to rethink bold!

Every corner's filled with art,
My cat's the ruler of this place,
He judges all; what a work of heart,
Flying furballs add to the grace!

On this path of quirk and jest,
I trip on thoughts and tumble wide,
But oh, each stumble feels like rest,
In here, I always take a ride!

Embraces Wrapped in Stillness

In comfy corners, silence sings,
But wait, a snore breaks that calm sound,
My partner's dreams of flying things,
While I sip tea and twirl around.

Huddled close on rainy nights,
Watching raindrops race and play,
With popcorn kernels taking flights,
I wonder if we'll save the day!

We've built our walls of cozy charm,
A fortress made of blankets bright,
Though tangled up, there's no alarm,
We seem to run on sheer delight!

In good company, silence feels loud,
Trading jokes that sometimes flop,
Yet in this stillness, I am proud,
Because our joys will never stop!

Thresholds Of Uncharted Feelings

Peeking through the door ajar,
What adventures lie in wait?
I glance down at a fun bazaar,
Filled with love, perhaps some fate!

Each doorway leads my heart to play,
Through ribbons bright and hats askew,
Stumbling forward in joy's ballet,
With every step, there's something new!

Navigating paths I never knew,
With silly sounds and prancing feet,
Each twist and turn pulls me askew,
Who knew this journey could be sweet?

Crossing thresholds makes me giddy,
With silly dances, not a care,
Laughing out loud, feeling pretty,
In this maze, I'm light as air!

Whispers in the Stillness

In a nook where giggles hide,
Socks and snacks take every stride.
Pillow forts and secret codes,
This laughter lane is where it explodes.

Dust bunnies dance, a clumsy crew,
They groan and tumble, it's true!
Tea parties for a stuffed bear grand,
They're the most refined in all the land.

The fridge sings songs of leftovers bold,
Each jar's a treasure chest of old.
Pickles with a side of glee,
A culinary mystery, indeed, for me!

In this quirky space, there's always room,
For silly faces and a heart that blooms.
Joy spills out, just like confetti,
In this sprinkled world, everything's ready!

Sanctuary of Secrets

Underneath the staircase small,
Lie treasures bold, forgotten, tall.
A secret stash of gummy bears,
And tales that float in empty chairs.

Clothes hang like ghosts in the breeze,
Whispering the snacks they tease.
Old board games with rules we've bent,
In this silly space, hours are spent.

Giggles echo from room to room,
As whispers fill the air with bloom.
Each corner holds a tale so sweet,
Where mischief waits for curious feet.

Unkempt blankets and pillows strung,
Voices of youth softly sung.
Each moment's brewed with a splash of fun,
In this sanctuary, we are never done!

Echoes of Affection

Walls tickle with laughter's light,
As shadows dance in pure delight.
Here we scribble our silly dreams,
In crayon outlines, bursting seams.

The clock chimes jokes at a funny hour,
As dust motes twirl in zany power.
Grandpa's stories never get old,
They turn to giggles, sweet and bold.

The cat lays sprawled, a furry king,
With cheeky meows that laugh and sing.
Our memories stick like paint on walls,
Echoing love through our joyful halls.

Toys have meetings, plotting their plays,
Chasing each other in the craziest ways.
In this cozy realm where chuckles thrive,
Our hearts will always feel alive!

Where Love Takes Root

In this garden where smiles bloom,
Laughter's fragrance fills the room.
A sprinkle of joy, a dash of cheer,
In quirky corners, love is near.

Bouncing balls and voices loud,
Form a cheerful, lively crowd.
The dog joins in with barking fits,
His furry antics, our best skits.

Underneath the table's edge,
Youthful hopes make their pledge.
Candy wrappers tell a tale,
Of sugary treasures we unveil.

In this nook, we plant our dreams,
Watered by giggles, or so it seems.
With laughter as roots, we grow so bright,
In this silly world, everything feels right!

Echoes of Warm Affection

In corners where laughter resides,
Socks dance and secrets confide.
A cat on the sofa, claims his throne,
Pudding cups reign, no need for a grown.

Bubble wrap pops like fireworks on cue,
Ignoring the rules that say, "Don't you do!"
Mismatched chairs tell stories, so bold,
In this realm of chaos, love's manifold.

Dishes sing songs, they clatter and cheer,
Funny shadows caper, bringing good cheer.
Oddball treasures, dust mites galore,
But the warmth in this place is what I adore.

Tapestry of Loneliness and Belonging

Stitched together with lonely seams,
Odd socks are the stuff of dreams.
Jigsaw puzzles missing a piece,
Yet somehow here, all worries cease.

A chair that creaks, a clock that tocks,
Houseplants plotting world domination, in flocks.
My neighbors complain about the noise,
Yet my heart sings loud, with uncontainable joys.

A lopsided rug, a dent in the wall,
Each flaw it seems just adds to the call.
Funny echoes return my delight,
In this quirky bubble, everything feels right.

Spectrums of Emotional Light

Sunlight spills through curtains askew,
Painting laughter in vibrant hues.
A toaster that pops with flair and a grin,
Sausages dance, as breakfast begins.

Jokes written in crayon on walls of beige,
Memories captured like text on a page.
A dog in a hat, oh what a sight,
In this carnival where heartbeats ignite.

Silhouettes sway to the tunes of the night,
As friends gather close, everything feels right.
Emotions flicker, like fireflies' flight,
In this rainbow of warmth, I shine so bright.

Windows Framed with Dreams

Windows that giggle with stories untold,
Peering outside, where adventures unfold.
A garden of gnomes, of mismatched styles,
With grins that stretch for endless miles.

The doorbell chimes in a tune out of tune,
While dishes spin round like a cartoon.
Squishy cushions and vibrant throws,
Where giggles bloom, and silliness grows.

Chasing reflections, we dance in a blur,
A parade of oddities, against every spur.
In this sanctuary of playful delight,
I've found the place where joy takes flight.

A Hearth of Memories

In the corner, sits a chair,
With a cushion like a bear.
I tell my secrets, it won't tell,
But sometimes it smells like toast as well.

Beneath the rug, there's a cat,
Who steals my socks, imagine that!
He guards our laughs, a furry knight,
Chasing shadows 'til the night.

The fridge hums a silly tune,
Once scared a ghost, or so they swoon.
It's stocked with snacks of every shade,
A treasure chest our hunger made.

Now here's the punch: our joy's like glue,
With pizza stains and laughter too.
In this space, where chaos reigns,
Every moment's light, no need for chains.

Walls Made of Embrace

The walls are painted in laughter's hue,
With spots of jelly and goo.
They listen close when whispers fly,
And join the dance when spirits sigh.

A picture hangs, it winks at me,
Of times we climbed a friendship tree.
Oh, the silly poses we did strike,
I'm convinced that two of us sweat like bikes!

When I trip over shoes at dawn,
The walls just chuckle, they won't yawn.
They hold the echoes of our games,
In this maze of hugs, love never tames.

So here's my vow, in this quirky den,
We'll sing and twirl, again and again.
These walls are soft as a warm embrace,
A circus space, our funny place!

The Cradle of Dreams

In the middle lies a well-worn bed,
Where dreams of chocolate dance in my head.
It bounces back when I'm full of cheer,
More springs than a rabbit, oh dear!

The walls are scribbled with all my plans,
Drawing adventures with silly crayons.
I swear I saw my teddy dance,
In pajama parties, they took a chance.

Every night the stars poke through,
They whisper tales, just like a crew.
With giggles bursting like fireflies,
Each dream a cake, with frosted skies.

So here's my shout to midnight's grace,
With quirky dreams, we'll lose all pace.
In this cradle of whimsy and fun,
We'll chase the laughter till we're done!

In the Charmed Nook

In the nook with cushions all around,
Where socks and laughter can be found.
We tell bad jokes and eat some fries,
As the clock giggles, time does fly.

A lamp with quirks, it flickers twice,
It's both a beacon and a vice.
The floorboards creak with laughter's glee,
As we jam to tunes in a offbeat spree.

With chaos reigning, we craft the fun,
Making memories like we're on the run.
In this space where silliness flows,
Who needs perfection? Of that, who knows!

So let's toast with mugs of cocoa warmth,
In this cozy spot, our hearts do swarm.
Adventure awaits beyond this nook,
With every page turned in our storybook!

Echoing Footsteps of Belonging

In squeaky shoes, we dance around,
Chasing echoes, lost and found.
With every step, the floorboard creaks,
Whispering tales that laughter speaks.

We trip on rugs, do somersaults,
Clumsily weaving through friendly faults.
In this chaos, joy is the guide,
With every tumble, our hearts collide.

Through swinging doors, we peek and prance,
Jumping into silliness at every chance.
There's comfort in each laughter's sound,
Together we're lost, yet always found.

With pizza boxes stacked so high,
We take aim, and, oh my, oh my!
Games and giggles linger in the air,
In this merry mess, we have no care.

Hearthside Stories of Old

Around the fire, we share our tales,
Of curious cats and silly snails.
Grandma's stories never grow old,
Like her knitted socks, warm and bold.

With marshmallow sticks aimed for the stars,
S'mores and giggles, oh, how bizarre!
The flames flicker, the shadows sway,
As we roast our puns alongside the play.

In cozy blankets, we snuggle tight,
Whispering secrets late into the night.
The popcorn pops, the stories flow,
With goofy grins and hearts aglow.

Even the dog dreams of the fun,
Chasing squirrels in dreams while we run.
In the glow of warmth, we find our space,
Sharing laughter, love, and a chocolate face.

Pockets of Peaceful Respite

In cushions soft, we find our nooks,
Stocked with snacks and funny books.
With pillows piled high like a fort,
We plot our next grand goofy sport.

A cup of cocoa, marshmallows afloat,
Reading comics, our brains remote.
Time stands still in this silly zone,
Where giggles echo, and quirks are grown.

Laughter bubbles like a fizzy drink,
In these pockets, we never think.
Creating moments, silly and bright,
In colorful chaos, we feel just right.

Whispers of dreams and adventures shared,
In these spaces, no one's compared.
A blend of joy, a dash of ease,
In the fun of friendship, we find our peace.

Flowing Rivers of Connection

Through winding paths of chuckles and cheer,
We paddle our boats, no hint of fear.
Skipping stones on the giggly stream,
In every splash, we find our dream.

With fishing poles made of candy canes,
We bait our lines with light-hearted grains.
The fish are tales, caught with ease,
Each one more silly, aiming to please.

Our laughter ripples, our hearts entwined,
In this playful flow, we're always aligned.
From quirky nooks to hidden bends,
In the river of fun, our journey never ends.

So let's sail on these waters wide,
With joy and laughter as our guide.
Together we float, together we dream,
In this funny current, we're a perfect team.

Palettes of Emotion

In a room of laughter, colors gleam,
Silly hats dance, they scheme and dream.
Joy spills over like paint in a rush,
Tickled pink in a hilarious hush.

Walls of giggles, ceilings of cheer,
Dancing like noodles, without any fear.
Comics hung up like art on display,
Each tickle of laughter is here to stay.

Bright orange moods and blue sappy days,
Pillows that chuckle in curious ways.
A canvas of quirks, a story untold,
Where humor is minted, and joy's made of gold.

Nestled in Solitude

In corners where quirkiness flickers and flares,
A cat wears a fedora, without any cares.
Jellybeans dance to the rhythm of time,
With socks that do cha-cha, a life so sublime.

Cushions that whisper, secrets of the day,
A teapot that giggles, when things go array.
The vase tells jokes with a crooked smile,
Keeping me chuckling, all the while.

A corner so cozy, yet wild and free,
Where solitude blooms, like a quirky old tree.
Each shadow a friend, with stories to share,
In a space where the silliness fills up the air.

Hearthstones of Hope

In the glow of the fire, marshmallows puff,
Squeaky chairs sing when the night gets tough.
Hope is a pie baked with whimsy and peace,
Where laughter is sprinkles that never do cease.

Doors creak like laughter that whispers and swell,
As dreams prepare stories they yearn to tell.
A spot for the silly, a place for delight,
With shadows that jiggle and dance in the night.

Each flickering ember ignites a good jest,
Like socks that go missing, which always perplex.
Gather 'round warmth, where joy's never far,
Beneath this bright mantle, we all are a star.

The Chamber of Resilience

Walls padded with giggles, a fortress of cheer,
Jokes in the wallpaper, laughter so near.
In this quirky chamber, we wobble and sway,
Finding resilience in silliness; yay!

Bouncing on cushions that mimic a grin,
Where each little tumble leads to a win.
Fumbles and blunders are welcomed as guests,
In this loveable chaos, we find our best.

With each little bump, we rise up anew,
Launching like rockets, just like we do.
For humor's a beacon, a light on our quest,
In this joyful chamber, we all feel blessed.

Embraced by Timelessness

In a cozy nook, time's on leave,
My socks are mismatched, don't you grieve.
With peanut butter spread on toast,
I'll be a breakfast champion, almost!

The cat's conducting with a paw,
While I'm losing chess, oh what a flaw.
The chair creaks loud, a musical score,
I laugh so hard, I almost roar.

Coffee stains on pages, a work of art,
Sketching my dreams, I play the part.
The clock's hands spin like a ballet,
In my funny realm, I'll dance all day.

With a smile so wide, I greet the day,
In my quirky world, I'll forever play.
Timeless moments wrapped in cheer,
Who needs to rush? Let's dawdle here!

Sighs of Solace

In my tiny lair, the walls are chatty,
The fridge hums tunes, and it's quite batty.
A teacup cracked, yet filled with dreams,
Sipping from it, all's never as it seems.

The goldfish swims in circles of thought,
While I ponder on battles I never fought.
A pizza slice thinks it's a pie,
Who knew emotions could get so high?

Laughter echoes, a silly song,
The vacuum's dancing, it won't be long.
As I munch popcorn, I laugh so loud,
Comfort's found in chaos, proud!

Amidst the clutter, I find my peace,
A world where nonsense will never cease.
Funny sighs of solace, here I dwell,
In a madcap habitat, all is well!

Dwelling of Whispered Dreams

Here in my space, dreams take a seat,
With ducks in bow ties that can't be beat.
A whispering breeze, it jokes with clouds,
Together we giggle, we laugh out loud.

The lamp's a comedian, bright and bold,
Spinning tales of kittens turned to gold.
I dance with shadows, a lively spree,
In this realm where logic doesn't agree.

Blankets piled up like a cozy fort,
Where marshmallows roam with a playful sort.
The window's a stage, curtains pulled wide,
As I take a bow to my quirky side.

Whispers dwell in this funny space,
Where dreams turn silly, a delightful race.
I chuckle with joy as I drift to sleep,
In this whimsical haven, my heart will keep.

Sanctuary of Silent Longings

In corners shy, where giggles hide,
I find my treasures, mischiefs abide.
Jellybeans scatter beneath the chair,
And the cat claims it all, without a care.

With socks thrown high, like flags of cheer,
I battle dust bunnies, oh dear, oh dear!
The couch unfolds like a slumbering king,
Where dreams fly high on laughter's wing.

Sighs float around on a pillow so plush,
Whispers of longing in a gentle hush.
My world's a circus, with me as the star,
Riding on comedy, my shining bizarre.

In this sanctuary, everything's bright,
Where silly takes flight, laughter ignites.
Silent longings turn to playful spree,
In this joyful refuge, I'll always be!

Hallways of Nostalgic Light

In halls where laughter echoes bright,
I trip on memories, what a sight!
A retro lamp flickers like a star,
Reminding me of who we are.

Dust bunnies dance in playful glee,
With socks from last Tuesday's spree.
The fridge hums a nostalgic tune,
While leftovers wait for a silver spoon.

Walls hold secrets, some quite tall,
The cat knows them; she judges all.
I swear that picture's moved again,
Or maybe it's just my silly brain.

So here's to this wacky, warm place,
Where every corner wears a face.
A waltz of quirks, a jolly spree,
My humble abode, so perfectly me.

Corners of Embraced Solitude

In corners where I find my peace,
I snuggle in as worries cease.
The vacuum hums its own sweet song,
While odd socks argue all night long.

A chair with lumps is my best friend,
With chipped armrests that slightly bend.
It's here I plot world domination,
While sipping weak coffee from my station.

The curtains sway with gentle cheer,
As if to whisper, "Stay right here!"
The fridge may grumble, bare and thin,
But snacks are rumored to be within.

So let the world spin wild outside,
In my cozy nook, I'll gently hide.
With giggles and sighs, it feels just right,
In corners where I embrace the night.

Roofs of Gentle Protection

Under a roof that leaks a bit,
I keep my plants, a jungle fit.
Umbrellas line the entrance way,
Each one a guide on rainy days.

The ceiling's got a drip or two,
But who needs showers? I got a view!
While squirrels host acrobatic shows,
Pretending not to eat my clothes.

Lightning bolts may dance around,
But inside, laughter's the only sound.
With pillows piled like giant hills,
And deck chairs that give me chills.

So when the skies grow dark and loud,
I nab my blanket, feel so proud.
With tales of warriors and knights so bold,
Under my roof, I am consoled.

Spaces of Eternal Affection

In spaces where hugs seem to bloom,
I twirl around in cheerful gloom.
The cat's delighted in the cheer,
While my plants pretend to hear.

A table set for tea and fun,
With mismatched cups, all quirks in one.
The cookies don't last half the time,
As laughter rolls like secret rhyme.

Photos hang like a family quilt,
With unearned pride and love we built.
Each smile's captured, forever cold,
In frames that are delightfully bold.

So here's to laughter, hugs, and cheer,
In this lively space, I hold you near.
With quirky moments, wild and bright,
We're bonded forever, through day and night.

Foundations of My Soul

In the cellar, moldy cheese,
We find treasures, if you please.
The floorboards creak with every step,
Echoes of secrets, promises kept.

Cracks in walls tell tales so bold,
Of dreams and laughter, bought and sold.
A sassy cat sits, judging me,
While I trip on socks and spill my tea.

The roof is leaky, rain drops fall,
Yet in this chaos, I stand tall.
With every wobble, and every quake,
I dance like no one's about to shake.

So here I build my little nest,
Where hope and humor are truly blessed.
Foundations shaky, but spirits high,
I laugh at life as clouds drift by.

Portraits on the Parlor Wall

The portraits stare with silly grins,
As they gossip 'bout my daily sins.
A painting of Grandma with a flex,
Yells, "Yoga! It's not just for specs!"

A grandpa with a funny hat,
Says, "Remember when you fell for that?"
These painted pals know every flaw,
With every chuckle, they drop my jaw.

Each frame a tale, a wink, a spin,
From when I tried to dance and spin.
"Oh child," they laugh, "you missed the beat!"
"But look at you, now that's a treat!"

So here I sit, with friends so true,
These portraits make a lively crew.
When life gets dull, I just take a glance,
And join the party—the ultimate dance!

Beams of Comfort

Sunbeams filter, through a crack,
Illuminating where I snack.
The couch, a throne, where I reside,
With crumbs galore, my loyal side.

A glow from windows, warm and bright,
Chasing shadows, chasing fright.
The cat purrs, a fuzzy ball,
As I binge-watch yet another fall.

With every spill and every stain,
Comfort finds me, joy remains.
The beanbag laughs, it's seen it all,
From snacks to naps, my favorite call.

So let the beams shine down on me,
In this cozy nook, I'm truly free.
With laughter and warmth around every bend,
Here's to the silliness that won't end.

The Room of Forgotten Laughter

In a corner, under a heap,
Lies a joke book, half-asleep.
It's laughing still, though without a sound,
Remnants of giggles all around.

Socks that match, a distant dream,
In here, chaos reigns supreme.
Toys from days when I wore a crown,
Now gather dust, in a goofy town.

Old photos stuck beneath the bed,
Remind me of all the things I said.
With each memory that I unearth,
Giggles come back, bringing mirth.

So I'll clean up this messy hall,
And recall the laughter, one and all.
For in this room, joy floats on air,
Forgotten laughter is everywhere.

Echoes in My Soul's Abode

In the attic, old socks hide,
With a cat that seems so spry,
It chases dust bunnies with pride,
Oh, how time does fly!

Echoes of laughter dance near,
A fridge that hums like a tune,
It spills secrets I hold dear,
Like a wacky afternoon.

Down in the cellar, I peek,
Where old chairs have made their stand,
Whispering tales in their creak,
As I munch on leftover candy, grand!

The walls wear memories like clothes,
Some vibrant and striped, others plain,
Through each crack, a story flows,
I giggle at the joy and pain.

Refuge of Resilient Hopes

In the corner, a plant thrives,
With leaves that wobble and sway,
It gives me the best high-fives,
Though it's not quite that way!

The couch is a ship, I declare,
Sailing the seas of my dreams,
With popcorn rations to spare,
In this land of make-believe schemes.

Pictures hang like funhouse art,
With smiles that stretch for miles,
Each face plays its quirky part,
Bringing out the silliest smiles.

Here, resilience takes a seat,
With cushions of laughter conjoined,
Every misstep tastes quite sweet,
As we dance in our weirdly coined.

Chambers of Unspoken Love

Under the bed, dust bunnies lurk,
With secrets they keep on file,
Some days they're better than work,
Making my heart crack a smile.

The kitchen sings with pots and pans,
Whistling tunes from breakfast cheer,
As I burn toast and make new plans,
Laughter pops like the toast's sheer.

In the hallway, shoes make their case,
Each step is a comedic feat,
They scuttle about with no grace,
As if tripping's their own funny beat.

Walls wear whispers and giggles bright,
Little moments they can invoke,
In this space, it feels just right,
Wrapped in moments that cherish the joke.

Foundations of Tender Memories

Here's a room where socks unite,
A mismatched dancing brigade,
From morning to late at night,
They shuffle in a sock parade!

The bathroom mirror grins at me,
Reflecting all my wild styles,
With toothpaste battles, we agree,
Each morning's filled with goofy smiles.

Stumbling through the doors of fate,
Hilarity hides in each nook,
Where laughter rolls up to create,
The pages of my favorite book.

In this abode, memories stack,
Like pancakes on a Sunday morn,
With laughter holding nothing back,
Who knew fondness could also be born?

Lattice of Intertwined Hearts

In a web of laughter, we quibble with glee,
Intersecting thoughts like buzzing bees.
When a sock goes missing, we stage a debate,
Is it the laundry or just our fate?

We dance on floors that creak like a song,
Twisting our tales, where do they belong?
A cat in a hat joins our silly parade,
Making mischief and plans to invade.

After pie fights, we scrub with a smile,
The noodles that splattered go out in style.
Every mishap just adds to the charm,
In our cozy haven, there's always a balm.

With butterflies painted on wallpaper bright,
We tell ghost stories that give quite a fright.
Yet laughter erupts, and the ghosts turn to jest,
In this tangled nest, we humor best.

Breezes of Serene Contemplation

A breeze tickles curtains, like whispers of fate,
As I ponder the metaphors on my plate.
Is pizza round? Or is it just a flat lie?
These thoughts float like clouds in a pastrami sky.

I sip lemonade, while icebergs of chill,
Drift past old thoughts that were quiet and still.
Do socks have feelings when left out to dry?
I swear one just winked—am I getting too spry?

The chair by the window creaks with delight,
Hearing dreams shared, glowing dreams at night.
Where lost keys chuckle and come back to stay,
Who knew pondering could light up the day?

On this quiet path, laughter leads the way,
In breezy contemplations, we lay back and sway.
Pondering life, in a giggle we trust,
For every deep thought, there's always a gust.

Stories of Timeworn Walls

The walls have ears—or so they all say,
Echoing stories from yesterday's play.
They groan with laughter at secrets once bold,
Of mishaps and shenanigans, all retold.

In crannies and corners, they store the jest,
Like that time I danced in my underwear fest.
The plaster might crack, but it's got a grin,
Holding dear chaos like a family sin.

With paintings askew, they offer no shame,
As we toast to our flaws, we all know our name.
Each ding tells a tale of a choice or a friend,
In this sanctuary, the fun never ends.

Like time-worn pillows, we gather and sigh,
Making new memories while whispering why.
In the embrace of these walls, we find our space,
To laugh at the quirky, the awkward, the grace.

Hearthstones of Shared Journeys

Around the fire, we gather and jest,
Each trip around the sun is a well-told quest.
With marshmallow stories that stick to our bones,
Our laughter ignites like the crackling stones.

We journey through snacks, through chaos, through games,
Inflating our tales, inflating our names.
Remember the time we mistook the cat?
For a mythical beast—imagine that spat!

As we toast to the future and roast all the s'mores,
Recalling our past as the laughter still soars.
With each bite of madness, we wander and roam,
Finding joy in the madness that feels just like home.

For every shared journey, both silly and bright,
Creates a collage of warmth in the night.
In the hearth's warm glow, every heart sings along,
As we dance to the rhythm of our shared, silly song.

Shadows of Longing

In the attic, dust bunnies dance,
They've thrown a party, they'll take a chance.
Old socks and shoes are mingling too,
I think they've invited a lost shoe crew.

The shadows whisper jokes from the wall,
While the fridge tells stories, standing tall.
I laugh with the shadows, a jolly good crowd,
What happens in here, we won't share aloud!

A cat plays poker with a chair,
All the while I wonder, do they care?
They place their bets with curled-up yarn,
Cheating's allowed; it's a funny charm!

Ghosts of laughter spill from each seam,
In this quirky place where I often dream.
I sigh at the wisdom these objects impart,
In the attic of wishes, they steal my heart.

The Garden of My Essence

In the backyard, gnomes guard my dreams,
They play hide and seek, or so it seems.
With my trusty weeds, I plant a grin,
While snails groove by, they're ready to win!

Sunflowers wear hats, singing off-key,
While tomatoes debate, 'who's juicier, me?'
The daisies gossip, spilling petal tea,
In this veggie world, laughter flows free!

I tried to water with soda once,
Now the garden's dancing—a fizzy bunce!
The carrots chuckle, "This is absurd!"
As I try to explain, my thoughts get blurred.

Each sprout's a buddy, bright in their stance,
They break into laughter with every chance.
In this garden alive with the weird and the zany,
I've found my patch, oh so crazy and rainy!

Corners Filled with Echoes

In every corner, whispers float by,
The toaster's gossip makes the bread cry.
Echoes of laughter bounce off the floor,
While the vacuum hums 'round every door!

Dust settles softly on unspoken tales,
Where old magazines tell of epic fails.
Pillows conspire in cozy delight,
Comfy debates last 'til the night!

Chairs swap secrets with worn-out shoes,
A sock puppet sings blues, with nothing to lose.
The refrigerator's cold jokes chill my spine,
While the echoing laughter is simply divine!

In this symphony of absurd things,
Chaos and humor, oh how it sings!
If you listen closely, you might just see,
Life is much better with echoes like these!

The Threshold of Tenderness

At the door, my pets gather 'round,
With wags and purrs, they make the sound.
Each welcome is loud, it's quite a parade,
In this fuzzy world, fears start to fade.

The doorbell rings, but they just stare,
Should we let it in? Nah, it's a spare!
With a twist and a shake, my cat takes a bow,
As if to declare, "Let's avoid him now!"

My heart's a doormat where laughter grows,
With each little paw and the scent of their woes.
They brew up warmth with their funny antics,
Turning mundane moments into romantic antics!

So here we stand, all snug and tight,
In a home full of giggles, everything's bright.
The threshold remains a sweet, silly place,
Where love and laughter always embrace.

Vaults of Untamed Imagination

In a kitchen made of candy, where cookies grow on trees,
I stir a pot of giggles, with a pinch of silly breeze.
The fridge hums tunes of laughter, ice cream sings at night,
And every time I open it, I'm greeted by delight.

There are bedrooms stuffed with pillow fights and sheets of rainbow bright,
Where the monsters in the closet hide, but never leave in fright.
A trampoline for dreams to bounce and soar without a care,
In vaults where whimsy dances, there is nothing we can't share.

My couch is made of marshmallows, soft and squishy too,
And every time I sit down, it gives a gentle woo-hoo!
Each corner holds a treasure, a hat or shoe askew,
In this realm of wild wonders, there's always room for two.

So come and join the laughter, let your worries fly away,
In this land of pure imagination, we'll play all night and day.
With every tale that's woven, our giggles intertwine,
Within these vaults of fancy, where the stars and dreams align.

Aisles of Reverent Silence

In the quiet of a library where whispers go to sleep,
The books all laugh in secret, their stories far too deep.
With words that dance like fireflies, and pages filled with cheer,
The aisles play hide-and-seek; come, let's explore them here.

Between the rows of novels, I trip on mismatched shoes,
The authors wave as I pass by, choosing which one to use.
A friendly ghost of Shakespeare winks as he turns his page,
While Down the Aisles of Reverent Silence, wild thoughts uncage.

A cat naps on the desk, with wisdom in its purr,
It guards the quiet treasures, each title a little blur.
And if you're very sneaky, you might just catch a peek,
Of dreams that leap like rabbits, in a world that's joyfully sleek.

So grab a book and giggle, let the stories take their flight,
In this playful sanctuary, nothing feels contrite.
Whispers turn to laughter, with each page we declare,
In the halls of whispered silence, joy is in the air!

Pillars of Unyielding Faith

In a living room of gumdrops, where silliness abounds,
The pillars stand spectacular, with laughter's joyful sounds.
They hold up all my wishes; they make my dreams so bold,
With colors bright and cheerful, a sight to behold.

Every wall a canvas of the colors that I choose,
A gallery of my wild thoughts, never colored by the blues.
On pillars made of giggles, my hopes spin round and round,
In this fortress of belief, happiness is found.

Like spaghetti made of sunshine, I twirl my silver fork,
And dance around the furniture, become a playful dork.
With every strum of laughter, the floors begin to sway,
These pillars keep me steady as I frolic and I play.

So let the world come rolling; I shall not lose my way,
In this sanctuary vibrant, where I can laugh and stay.
With every goofy moment, faith rises high above,
In the structure of my joy, there's only room for love.

Lights of Guiding Presence

In a hall of twinkling lanterns, where shadows dance with glee,
The lights are all my buddies, they sparkle just for me.
They flicker with a secret, a joke they softly hum,
And lead my silly footsteps, to where the fun is from.

Each glow bulb is a friend, cheering with a dainty wink,
They light the path of laughter, in puddles where we sink.
The chandeliers are spinning tales of joy throughout the night,
While we bounce to the rhythm, in a glow of pure delight.

The night sky's full of giggles, as the stars join in the fun,
With moonbeams weaving stories, and a smile from the sun.
The lights above keep shining, guiding hearts like ours,
In this carnival of silliness, we celebrate the stars.

So come and dance together, let the brightness never end,
In this space of glowing magic, let our spirits freely blend.
With every jig and wiggle, joy's the treasure that we send,
In the lights of guiding presence, laughter is our friend.

A Skylight of Serenity

In a corner, a cat does nap,
Dreams of fish and a lovely lap.
The toaster sings a morning tune,
While slippers dance in the afternoon.

Coffee brews with a gurgling shout,
The refrigerator starts to pout.
A curtain flutters, a playful breeze,
As the light spills in with lazy ease.

Lampshades wobble with a slight cheer,
Echoes of laughter ring crystal clear.
The wallpaper with polka dots,
Whispers secrets of all the plots.

As socks vanish, I take a stand,
In this wild and quirky land.
With giggles bouncing off the walls,
Home is where the funny calls.

The Pathway to Belonging

Shoes in a row, they love to play,
One's always gone, oh what a hey!
Each step is filled with silly dance,
As a broomstick grants a twirling chance.

The doormat greets with a cheeky grin,
Here comes the dog with a squeaky win.
He rolls in dirt, and he's so proud,
While we laugh, even when he's loud.

The doorbell rings, it's time for fun,
Neighbors gather, oh what a run!
With cookies flying and jokes on tap,
Together we share a hearty clap.

Through each hallway, stories bloom,
A rug that giggles, a sweet perfume.
In this lively maze, we find delight,
Home is a party, from morning to night.

Stillness Beneath the Eaves

Beneath the eaves, the spiders weave,
Tales of mischief, you won't believe.
A snail steals chocolate, oh what a treat,
While dust bunnies dance to a jazzy beat.

The clock does tick with a silly face,
Wobbling along in a frantic race.
The shadows fall in comical ways,
Socks on the ceiling, a strange malaise.

Cushions conspire, plotting their rest,
Laughing at humans who think they're best.
As cushions giggle and pillows peek,
Home's a riot, not for the meek.

Dust motes twirl, so light and spry,
Echoing laughter as they drift by.
Stillness hums with a joyous tune,
In corners where happiness begins to bloom.

Remnants of Joy

Crumbs on the floor tell a story bright,
Of snacks consumed in mid-movie flight.
The couch wears stains of laughter and cheer,
Remnants of joy from yesteryear.

A forgotten shoe spies from beneath,
Its twin long lost, a tale of beneath.
The coffee spills in a graceful arc,
Artistic chaos, a modern mark.

In the cabinet, a teapot sings,
Of fanciful tea parties and royal flings.
Lights flicker as if in a jest,
Inviting us all to a merry fest.

With each giggle, the walls shake and sway,
Creating a beat for the dance of play.
So we gather close, in this merry land,
With remnants of joy, forever grand.

Scrolls of Heartfelt Confessions

In the attic, dust collects,
My secrets bound with tape and text.
The cat knocks over all my plans,
While I sip tea from wobbly cans.

Notes of love and cringe-worthy lines,
Scrawled in ink, mixed with some wines.
The paper trails of what I've said,
Reveals my crush on the neighbor's shed.

Late-night ramblings, a snicker or two,
Tales of my life like a blooper reel, it's true.
If walls could laugh, they'd burst with glee,
At the chaos that lives inside of me.

In this clutter, I find my gaffe,
A comedian's life, just let it laugh.
With every stumble, I learn to mend,
The jester's crown is my dearest friend.

Whispers Beneath the Eaves

In the corners, shadows creep,
Where memories giggle, never sleep.
They argue with echoes of yesteryear,
While I'm searching for my lost career.

The squirrels chatter, plotting schemes,
Stealing dreams, or so it seems.
With every rustle, my curtains flare,
Like they're playing hide and seek in despair.

My coffee pot's a gossip queen,
Bubbling tales of things unseen.
Pass the sugar for those sweet tales,
As laughter lifts like paper sails.

A symphony of clatter and cheer,
Where every mishap brings good-natured sneer.
So I'll laugh with the buds on this tree,
In the whispers where humor sets me free.

Skylights of Infinite Possibility

Through glass above, the sunbeam slides,
Awakens hopes, where silliness hides.
The birds audition for the morning show,
Chirping their tunes, putting on a glow.

Beneath the clouds, my plans do swirl,
A dreamer's trap, with twirls and twirls.
A trampoline of colors up so high,
Jumping for joy and trying not to cry.

Chairs start dancing, windows shake,
As I contemplate my next mistake.
The ceiling fans are rhythm kings,
Spinning tales of all the joy life brings.

Let's toast to life with juice or tea,
Embracing chaos, wild and free.
With skylights open, let laughter in,
In this remarkable place where dreams begin!

Bridges of Kindred Spirits

On creaky planks, we trek along,
Singing off-key, a joyful song.
My friends are quirks in each step we take,
Creating memories, through every mistake.

With mismatched socks and silly hats,
We share the treasures of our spats.
Puns fly like kites in the frosty air,
Each giggle echoes, but we don't care.

Through laughter's path, our hearts entwine,
Building bridges, one joke at a time.
Like rickety rails that stretch afar,
We find our strength in who we are.

So here's to us, the wobbly crew,
With heartbeats synced, and a love so true.
We'll dance like no one's watching near,
On bridges made of laughter and cheer.

Quilt of Warmth

In cozy corners cookies bake,
With crumbs that dance and giggle awake.
The cat's on the couch, a furry champ,
While socks explode in a laundry camp.

The laughter bubbles like a boiling pot,
With mishaps and joy, we've got quite a lot.
Each patch of fabric tells a good tale,
Of silly adventures where we set sail.

Whiskers twitching, the dog's in the fray,
Chasing his tail like it's a great play.
Under this quilt, all fits right,
In our silly world, oh what a sight!

So gather around, let's knit a few dreams,
With stitches of laughter and playful schemes.
Each thread's a memory, worn and bright,
A quilt full of warmth, our hearts take flight.

Lanterns of Reminiscence

Beneath the glow of evening's light,
We dance with shadows, oh what a sight!
With lanterns swinging, we tell our tales,
Of epic fails and of ridiculous trails.

The garden gnomes, in silly repose,
Listen and chuckle, we share our woes.
Bumpy bike rides with seats that squeak,
We laugh at our past with rosy cheeks.

Ghosts of lost socks remember their mates,
In a whimsical world where no one waits.
Every lantern glows like a smile so wide,
Guiding us through life's crazy ride.

So let the flickers spark up delight,
Beneath these lanterns, everything's right.
We celebrate quirks, with laughter's sweet balm,
In a kingdom of memories, forever calm.

The Attic of Wishes

Up in the attic, with boxes piled high,
Are dreams and dust bunnies, oh me, oh my!
A kite from the past begs to take flight,
While old dolls gossip on a starry night.

A top hat rolls by with a whimsical spin,
Where every adventure might just begin.
Wish lists forgotten, now tangled in yarn,
Sing tales of grandeur, and some slight yarns.

Old games sit waiting, their pieces askew,
With stories of laughter still ringing true.
In this odd nook, where memories blend,
Each dusty trinket feels like an old friend.

So peek through the keyhole of what used to be,
In a world where wishes come wild and free.
For magic's still here in each creaky floor,
In the attic of wishes, let's explore!

Footsteps on Familiar Floors

Every footstep echoes in a big ol' way,
From kitchen to hallway, we frolic and play.
With rubber ducky serenades and laughter's hum,
We skip 'round the house, and waddle like a duck!

The floors creak like a marching band on parade,
As silly shenanigans switch up our trade.
We try new dances, our feet out of sync,
With giggles and smiles, we'll never rethink.

In the hallway, the dog leads the way,
His furry tail wagging as if to say,
"Join in the frolic; let's spin and twirl,"
Round and round, in our magical whirl.

Through every room, joyous laughter flows,
With knick-knacks and memories in unending rows.
So let's dance on these floors, oh what a score,
With footsteps and tickles, we always want more!

Landscapes of Heartfelt Desire

In the garden, weeds do dance,
A flower's wiggle finds romance.
Squirrels debate the best tree seat,
While neighbors argue over peat.

Bees buzz tunes of silly glee,
While butterflies sip, 'Oh, let it be!'
Sunflowers twist to catch a glance,
Love's in bloom—give weeds a chance!

Rain drops join the fun parade,
Each puddle's splash—a grand charade.
A cat and dog compete in race,
But both get stuck in muddy grace!

The breeze whispers tales of cheer,
Even the fence post joined the sphere.
In this land of laughter bright,
Heartfelt dreams take joyful flight.

Anchors of Unshakeable Bonds

Two chairs rock, they creak in sync,
Bonded by gossip and a clink.
Grandpa's tales of fish so bold,
While Grandma's yarns make kids feel old.

A dog drags in the muddy mess,
'Twas not me!' he barks, trying to impress.
The anchor tight—a toddler's hug,
Family ties warm like a snug rug.

Spaghetti nights, sauce on the wall,
Everyone's laughter echoes the hall.
Each silly mishap brings a cheer,
Bonds grow strong with every year.

In this ship, love is the sail,
Navigating storms makes us prevail.
Though anchors weigh, they never tire,
Together, we rise—our hearts catch fire!

Gables of Ancestral Love

Old gables shuffle under the moon,
Whispers of stories make them swoon.
A creaky floor sings a tune so sweet,
While shadows dance on worn-out feet.

Grandma's cookies leave a trail,
Of crumbs and laughter, no way to fail.
The attic holds hats of silly past,
Each one's history is meant to last.

In every corner, a ghost may grin,
As family photos gather in.
A cheeky smile, a wink from the frame,
Ancestral love—never quite the same!

Yet in these walls, we roam and play,
Each echo sings, "Come join the fray!"
In the gables where love will thrive,
We find our roots—oh, how we jive!

Ripples of Enduring Trust

A pond reflects the sky's blue dance,
Frogs leap in with a splendid prance.
Each splash sends ripples, oh so wide,
Trusting old turtles to bide their stride.

Ducklings waddle in a silly line,
Trust in their mother—a task divine.
Each twist and turn—oh what a thrill,
The water giggles, a giddy chill.

In this pool of playful vibes,
Friendships grow like the finest scribes.
Silly fish race with little doubt,
In this trust, we laugh and shout!

So let your heart be like gentle waves,
In ripples of joy, love saves.
For here we learn, of bonds so sweet,
In every splash, our lives repeat!

www.ingramcontent.com/pod-product-compliance
Lightning Source LLC
Chambersburg PA
CBHW070312120526
44590CB00017B/2651